Wealth Accumulation Made Simple and Easy

Personal Finance
Wealth Accumulation Is a Mindset
The Basics for Your Investment Journey
A Must-Read for the Beginner and Midlevel Investor
Everything You Need to Know about Investing in One Place

Esau Williamson

ISBN 979-8-88685-319-3 (paperback)
ISBN 979-8-88685-538-8 (hardcover)
ISBN 979-8-88685-320-9 (digital)

Copyright © 2023 by E&R Williamson Enterprises LLC

All rights reserved. No part of this publication may be reproduced, distributed, or transmitted in any form or by any means, including photocopying, recording, or other electronic or mechanical methods without the prior written permission of the publisher. For permission requests, solicit the publisher via the address below.

Christian Faith Publishing
832 Park Avenue
Meadville, PA 16335
www.christianfaithpublishing.com

Printed in the United States of America

I dedicate this book to my late mother, Arreather Williamson, who instilled the many traits in me that have had a profound positive impact on my life; my wife, Rosa Maria Williamson; and our children, Esau II, Alexander, Jennifer, and their families. You are the light of my life.

Chapter 1

Wealth Accumulation Mindset

Let the fun begin. The United States is a capitalistic society full of opportunities to grow personally, professionally, spiritually, and, yes, financially. Even with the unlimited opportunities to excel, many Americans or so it appears are not able to participate to the fullest in the benefits of living in a capitalistic society with such great opportunities as that of the United States. People of color and females seem to bear the major impact of not participating in the unlimited opportunities available in the United States, which puts these families at greater risk of not succeeding financially. Whites are impacted as well as people of color but at a much lower rate. Nothing seems to work completely to bring many families out of poverty and low economic status except extensive federal government social programs. Our two major political parties can't agree and have not been willing to support the many social programs that would be required to assist families to get above the poverty line and others to the middle class as evidenced by the recent failure of the Build Back Better plan. Many Americans work two or three jobs yet can't seem to make the financial progress required to get to a comfortable financial position.

People stuck in these less fortunate financial positions need assistance from those of us who can show them the road to a more successful financial future. Low income may be a factor, but it's not the only factor. People have a tendency to spend what they make regardless of income level. Many or most middle-class Americans have not been able to crack this nut and excel financially. Feedback we often receive in the financial services world from people who could have set aside dollars for their future is "I wish I had gotten started saving and investing sooner." This statement has had a profound impact on me, and it showed me I needed to do more. My desire is for everyone to get what they need and start a financial plan upon entering the workforce even though it's never too late to get started. These are among the reasons I am writing this book.

The mission of this book is to ensure everyone has a basic understanding of how to get to a much better financial position regardless of your current situation. You should get started sooner rather than later. Finances are a personal decision, one that places significant stress on the majority of individuals, marriages, and significant other relationships. Oftentimes you will find a spender and a saver in relationships. It may appear the two are at odds when a little preplanning could bring an acceptable solution to the family feud. The key solution is to agree on a budget. Compromise is in order here. In other words, it's okay to live an abundant life when you can afford it without jeopardizing your future financial situation. It is paramount that you save first and then spend. Otherwise, you may overspend and put your future abundant financial situation in jeopardy.

This book will outline some of the basic tools and strategies that will educate everyone on how you can be more successful financially. Wealth accumulation is simple and easy, yet most people never get started on a simple financial plan to put themselves on track to achieve a better financial position. Let's dispel the myth that you must be born into wealth to be successful financially. Nothing is further from the truth. Everyone, regardless of current financial situation, can accumulate assets and achieve a better financial position.

Throughout my career as a financial advisor, many people have asked me, "If it's so simple and easy to get on track to a better financial position, why isn't everyone doing it?" That's a great question, and no one has a definitive answer to this question. I believe part of the issue is probably due to a lack of knowledge and education. This book is designed to address the basic lack of knowledge issue, but it's not enough. The broad general answer is our education systems need to be revamped and provide personal finance courses as part of the required curriculum. I believe a major part of the real answer is "It's a mindset." Most people simply don't believe they can get to a better financial position because of their current financial situation. Excuses pile on here: "I must make more money," "I never can see myself out of my current financial situation," "I have too much debt, my student loans," "It's someone else's fault I'm in this financial position," etc. Hold on a minute. If you are convinced you can't succeed financially, it probably won't happen.

Let's consider the mindset of professional ballplayers. No one knows for sure whether you will become a professional ballplayer. We do know one of the first steps is to believe you can. Then, it takes lots of coaching, practice, and playing time over years and years and even decades to get there. You, like the professional ballplayer, must have a positive can-do mental attitude. Simply put, you must believe and know that you can succeed. Then, realize it won't happen overnight. Wealth accumulation is not a quick get-rich scheme. It's a marathon, not a sprint. You must understand it will take years and years and even decades to achieve financial success.

This shift in mindset requires you to believe and understand that a part of what you earn should be set aside for your future. You cannot spend everything you earn over a long period of time and expect to be in a better financial position in the future. You must learn to spend less than what you earn. My mother used to say when we were little, "If you have a dime, spend a nickel and save a nickel." This statement has remained with me my entire life. While I couldn't save half of what I earned, I did make it a priority to set aside money for the future. You will also learn in this book why I would modify the statement my mother taught us: if you have a dime, spend a nickel, save 2¢, and invest 3¢. Investing allows you to participate in the growth of this great nation and the companies that make this sustained growth possible. You must invest to significantly increase the probability of financial success. We live in a capitalistic society and have the opportunity to participate in its future growth just like the wealthiest Americans do. A solid financial plan can bring families across the poverty line, others clearly into the middle class, and middle-class Americans to the upper class and keep you there, forever and ever.

While this book will not make you a master investor, it will introduce you to proven concepts and techniques to get on track and stay on track to achieve a better financial position. It will show you how simple and easy it is to get to a better financial position. Hopefully, these simple and easy tools and techniques will give you the mindset that you believe you can achieve financial success. Once you are confident that you can get to a better financial position, it will happen. The tools, strategies, and techniques outlined in this book will give you the basic understanding and hopefully the confidence to start and continue your financial journey. Additionally, consider engaging a professional financial advisor as soon as you have the opportunity to work with one.

Financial firms and financial advisors have target markets in which they choose to engage. Many financial firms and financial advisors have income, net investable assets requirements, or both before they will consider working with you. Financial advisors bring great value to the relationship and can assist you to accumulate even greater wealth. Use the Financial Industry Regulatory Authority's website (https://brokercheck.finra.org) or the Securities and Exchange Commission's website, (https://adviserinfo.sec.gov) to learn more about your financial advisor and broker firm.

This book is designed for beginner and midlevel investors to answer many of your questions so you can get started or increase your savings and investments today. You should consider three separate but related pillars as you begin your quest for a better financial position: risk management, savings, and wealth management. We will take a close look at each of these three pillars separately and address why each is important. Please note it is beyond the scope of this book to address risk management in great detail. However, we must review risk management briefly because without the proper insurance in place, your financial plan may be derailed in the event of an accident or incident that requires significant funds.

Suggested Action Now: Develop a positive mindset to overcome obstacles as required and start or enhance your long-term financial plan upon completion of reading this book.

Chapter 2

Budget

A budget is the required first step in putting together a financial plan regardless of how small or large. A budget allows you to determine precisely the dollars available to fund a financial plan. This is a moment where you want near-exact science to take over and reveal where the money is going. A budget is not about reducing your fun, beer, or shopping money; it's about determining where your money is going, which affords you the opportunity to make appropriate adjustments and free up additional dollars for your financial plan. It's your decision and yours alone.

A budget is the tool to diagnose the status of your financial affairs and therefore requires a thorough examination. A budget must track all income coming into the household and its use once identified. Keep it simple. You can search the Web for a personal budget template or use the website below. A budget template will simplify the budget process.

A budget will enable you to see the true value of your household income. Most families never get the luxury of experiencing the benefits of their entire income because a large portion of their income is dedicated to debt payments to pay off past purchases and perhaps an excessive percentage of income is going to entertainment. Excessive funds dedicated to entertainment can cripple your chances of getting to a much better financial position. Create a budget and determine where your hard-earned money is going.

Once established, get accustomed to living on your monthly budget and stick to it as much as possible. During our discussion on savings in chapter 5, I will share with you how to manage unforeseen expenses so they do not interfere with your established budget and monthly cash flow. Some may decide that there are no free dollars or not enough dollars available to start a financial plan. That may be true, but let's take a closer look.

Having trouble finding money in the budget to fund your financial plan? Having trouble determining where your hard-earned dollars are going? Here's a simple technique to assist you to fine-tune your budget and identity funds to get started on your financial journey.

- o Keep track of what you spend during any consecutive thirty-day period. Both spouses must participate. Put a notepad in your purse or pocket or keep track electronically. Log all expenditures that cost $1 or more.
- o Review your expenditures at the end of the thirty-day period and determine what adjustments you can make. Are there any expenditures you can reduce or eliminate? For example, let's assume you eat out for lunch and purchase a gourmet coffee each workday; $7 lunch + $3 coffee = $10 per day × 21 or 22 workdays per month; expenditures add up very quickly. An adjustment would be to take lunch from home two or three days a week and reduce cash outlay. Reduce the amount in half, for example, and increase the funds available to start your savings and investment plans.
- o This is just one brief example of how to make acceptable adjustments when finalizing your budget.

There are many budget templates on the Internet that you can download and use. Or use the Make a Budget Worksheet template on the Federal Trade Commission website (https://consumer.gov) to complete a simple budget. Again, please note we are not trying to take away your fun, shopping, and beer money, just encouraging better use of the funds that are available to you.

Suggested Action Now: Develop a budget and determine how much you can afford to contribute to your financial plan. Then, stick to your budget.

Chapter 3

Debt Management

Debt management goes hand in hand with your established budget. Keeping a good handle on your budget and debt is essential to putting yourself in a good position to start and continue to fund a financial plan appropriately based on your household income. Excessive debt and an unbalanced budget will spell trouble short-term and long-term. Get out of debt and enjoy all the benefits of your household income.

All your recurring payments should be included in your budget and managed so debt payments do not exceed a certain percentage of your income, which we will address shortly in this chapter. It's appropriate to buy large ticket items on credit and make recurring payments over time to pay for them. One important factor is to not make too many purchases on credit at the same time and pile up excessive debt and recurring payments. Consider delaying some of your purchases so you don't overextend credit. For example, a newlywed couple upon purchasing a four-bedroom home probably would like to fully furnish the entire house immediately. Four bedrooms, kitchen, dining room, living room, and a thousand other purchases at once may be too much for the budget initially. So why not consider purchasing furniture for one or two or even three bedrooms (bedrooms furnished for the parents and in-laws to visit) initially? Then, purchase additional furnishings upon paying off some of your initial loans. The freed-up capital from paying off some of your current debt will now be available to make the monthly recurring payments on your new purchases. This is just an example of managing debt and avoiding excessive debt payments at once.

Do not overextend credit; it can be hazardous to your financial well-being. You should work extremely hard to keep all your recurring debt payments including your house payment to no more than 40% of your gross household income, also known as your debt-to-income ratio. This way you are almost assured to qualify for loans as needed unless there are other extenuating circumstances that affect your credit, such as a previous bankruptcy or excessive unsecured debt. For example, let's assume both spouses work and each spouse makes $3,000 per month for a total of $6,000 gross household monthly income. $6,000 × 40% = $2,400. Your total fixed recurring monthly payments shouldn't exceed $2,400. Some financial institutions may consider a 45% debt-to-income ratio depending on the financial institution's standard operating procedures and your total financial picture.

Secured vs. Unsecured Debt

Another important factor financial institutions will consider when determining whether to approve your loan request is how much unsecured debt you have. Secured debt is backed by property, such as home loans, car loans, etc. If you default on a secured loan, the financial institution can repossess the secured item, such as your car or foreclose on your house. Then, the financial institution can sell these items to pay off the balance of the loan you owe. Unsecured debt is nothing more than a promise to repay the loan. Credit card debt and personal signature loans are examples of unsecured debt. If you default on an unsecured loan, there is nothing for the financial institution to repossess to pay off the balance of your loan. Each financial institution will have an unsecured debt limit they will accept to approve your loan requests. For example, if you have more than $10,000 in unsecured debt, the financial institution may not approve your loan until the unsecured debt balance is below a stated amount.

Credit Cards

Credit cards are very much a part of our normal everyday financial lives and are unsecured debt. Appropriate and selected use of credit cards is great and limits the pain associated with paying for purchases in person and online. It's okay to have one or two credit cards, but limit your purchases. Very importantly, pay your credit card balances in full each month whenever possible. If you have revolving credit card debt, design a strategy to pay off the credit card balances as quickly as possible to avoid paying high interest associated with credit cards.

The overuse of credit cards can be detrimental to your financial health. Credit cards charge high to very high compound interest rates that can have a significant impact on your monthly budget and cash flow. You want to enjoy high compound interest rates on your investments but not on your credit cards. Paying high credit card interest rates works for financial institutions to increase their profitability but not for you. Credit cards can be used to make purchases during the month, but pay the balance in full each month to avoid paying high interest rates on your purchases. For example, if you use your credit card to pay for groceries during the month, save the cash you would have paid on the spot and pay the bill in full and on time to avoid paying any interest. This is an appropriate use of your credit cards and will not cost you any additional out-of-pocket fees. Also, consider using debit cards to make purchases and avoid credit card use as much as possible. Debit cards provide the convenience of a credit card, but it's a cash purchase because the cash comes directly out of your bank account just like writing a check.

Selecting the Right Credit Cards

You need to know how to compare credit cards and select the right credit card(s) for you. You want to select credit cards with the lowest interest rate and fees, which can be confusing. Financial institutions must provide you with the annual percentage rate or APR, which takes into account annual fees (if any) and interest rates. All financial institutions must inform you of the credit card APR prior to you applying for a credit card. Comparing APRs on credit cards is an apple-to-apple comparison. Generally, you want to select credit cards with the most favorable APR unless you have a valid reason to choose a different card, such as the credit card awards program.

Make Recurring Payments on Time

Pay all bills on time every time, period. Paying bills on time every time will increase your credit score. Higher credit scores will assist you to qualify for loans and lower the interest rates financial institutions will charge you. Make more than the minimum payment if you can afford to do so to reduce the time it takes to pay off loans. Paying minimum payments will almost certainly guarantee that you will pay significantly more in interest and sometimes to the extent that the interest paid exceeds your initial loan amount. Look at your credit card statements and review the devastating impact of making minimum payments.

Debt Consolidation Loans

A lower-interest debt consolidation loan can be a saving grace to get out of high-interest loans and credit card debt. You should have a relationship with a bank or credit union to address your banking needs. If not, establish a relationship with one promptly. Banks and credit unions offer debt consolidation loans with very favorable interest rates to allow you to consolidate balances on high-interest credit cards and other loans. Many financial institutions will allow you to use your nontax-qualified savings and investment accounts as collateral to further reduce the interest rates on debt consolidation loans. Debt consolidation loans are a good way to reduce high-interest-rate loans and free up cash that can be used to get out of debt sooner and fund your financial plan. Consider a debt consolidation loan as necessary.

Review information about credit card interest rates on the Federal Deposit Insurance Corporation (FDIC) website (www.fdic.

gov). Once debt is under control, the next step is to address the three pillars of a financial plan: risk management, savings or banking, and wealth management.

Suggested Action Now: Develop a strategy and start paying off debt.

Chapter 4

Risk Management

Risk management is a very important part of every financial plan and should be viewed as a necessity and not a luxury item. Risk management is nothing more than deciding which risks you choose to keep and which risks you choose to transfer to an insurance company by paying an insurance premium. Risk management is purchasing the many types of insurance needed to protect you and your family in the event of an accident, sickness, mishap, or loss of life. For example, if you own an automobile, you should have auto insurance to cover you in the event of an accident. The deductible you choose when purchasing auto insurance is an example of retaining risk. You can lower your deductible by paying a higher insurance premium, or you can elect to pay a lower premium, which will increase your deductible. *It is important to note that insurance must be purchased before you need it. If you wait until you need insurance, you may not be able to purchase it.* If you have auto insurance prior to an accident, your insurance company will cover the accident up to the amount of insurance you purchased minus your deductible. If you don't have auto insurance at the time of the accident and purchase insurance afterward, the insurance company will not cover the accident because the accident occurred before the effective date of the insurance purchased. All insurance works this way. You must own it before you need it, or you won't be covered in the event of an accident or incident.

Here are a few common types of insurance that most families may need at some point and you should consider as you put your financial plan together. Here's a brief description of each:

- Health insurance—to cover medical costs if you or your family members get sick or hospitalized.
- Life insurance—used to pay final expenses associated with death. Very importantly, life insurance provides lump-sum payments to beneficiaries in the event of death to ensure loved ones have sufficient funds to maintain a reasonable standard of living, college education funds for children, and many other requirements under such circumstances.
- Disability insurance—provides income to workers in the event of temporary or permanent disability.
- Long-term care insurance—used to pay for assistance when help is needed with the basic activities of daily living.
- Automobile insurance—insurance to cover expenses associated with an automobile accident. Liability coverage will pay for bodily injuries and property damage if you are responsible for the accident. Your automobile insurance may provide minimum medical coverage for injuries sustained in an accident.
- Homeowner insurance—insurance to cover your home in the event perils occur, such as fire or theft. Liability coverage provides protection for injuries to others and property damage. Provides medical coverage for others not living in the household in the event of an accidental injury.
- Renter's insurance—insurance to cover your personal property when you are not the homeowner.
- Umbrella insurance—umbrella insurance policies provide additional liability coverage above the liability insurance limits in other policies, such as your auto and homeowner insurance policies. Umbrella insurance may also provide liability coverage not covered by your other policies.

WEALTH ACCUMULATION MADE SIMPLE AND EASY

Risk management protects you when an unforeseen event occurs and must be an integral part of everyone's quest for financial success. Without the proper risk management products in place, the out-of-pocket costs associated with an incident may set you back an entire lifetime and prevent you from achieving your financial goals.

A financial advisor can assist you to do an analysis to help determine your family's risk management needs.

Suggested Action Now: Review your family's need for the different types of insurance and purchase appropriate coverage as required.

Chapter 5

Savings

Are you ready to have some fun? We have finally arrived at the exciting parts of a financial plan—savings and investments. The savings pillar is designed to address your short-term needs for cash and is a key component in everyone's journey to get to a much better financial position. When the unexpected need for cash occurs, you must have cash at your disposal. Or you may be forced to take out a loan, use credit cards and can't pay off the balance promptly, or even have to liquidate assets in perhaps an unfavorable market or some other unfavorable option. It doesn't matter what your reason is. You either have cash or you don't. The wealthiest of Americans, oftentimes, have enormous sums of cash in savings because they are aware that at some point, they are going to have a greater need for cash than what comes in via their regular monthly cash flow. All Americans are aware of these unforeseen events that affect all of us at some point or another, yet most people never seem to put a plan in place to adequately address these inevitable short-term contingencies that plague a simple but comprehensive financial plan. The mission of this book is to change this scenario and make sure everyone has access to the basic information you need so you can stop delaying the right thing to do. The right thing to do is start saving or increase your savings to an appropriate percentage of your income. The mission of savings is to enhance your financial situation promptly. For this reason and many others, some consider the savings pillar to be the most important link that holds a financial plan together. Let's explore why.

If you don't have money in savings to take care of contingencies, you probably will have to interrupt your long-term investments and use those funds for other than what they were designed to do. Worse yet, you may use credit cards and not be able to pay off the balance each month. This means you are paying high credit card interest rates, which will impede your ability to save and invest and continue your quest for a better financial position.

Let's address two types of savings: emergency savings and contingency savings. You must set aside dollars for both emergencies and contingencies.

True emergencies deal with sickness or death in the family and require funds for you to deal with these types of situations in a timely manner. Short-term contingencies will happen throughout your lifetime, and you must be prepared to address them. So what are these short-term contingencies? They are things that will happen due to wear and tear and unforeseen mishaps—for example, new tires for your automobile, the furnace breaking and needing repair or replacing, broken windows, automobile accidents, vacations, etc.

Plan for the unexpected. You want to have sufficient funds available to deal with all contingencies above your normal monthly cash flow expenses. Therefore, you must dedicate sufficient funds to savings each month or payday to ensure this key feature works as designed. I recommend you establish a savings goal of 3–5% of your pay initially. Set up an automatic transfer of 3–5% of your pay to go to your savings account each payday. This is called paying yourself first. While you may not be able to start at this rate initially, get started at whatever level and make it a goal to get there as soon as possible as you pay off debt and free up cash flow and receive promotions and pay raises. The money going to savings will be used to pay unforeseen bills when an emergency or contingency occurs. You won't know in advance what the funds will be used for until a mishap occurs. When a mishap occurs, savings is the pool of money that is readily available to address the emergency or contingency. Therefore, adequate funds in savings are crucial and an essential part of your financial journey to financial success.

How Much Should You Have in Savings?

There are many schools of thought as to how much money you should have in savings. Many financial advisors recommend between three and six months' pay in savings to take care of true emergencies and contingencies. For example, in the event of a job change, it may take you three to four months to find acceptable employment. Your savings will help bridge the expense gap to make ends meet until you are employed again.

You can combine emergency and contingency savings in one account if you have the discipline to not spend your emergency savings on contingencies. If not, set up two separate savings accounts and separate your emergency and contingency funds.

A question that may eventually arise is, What if we are fortunate and do not experience an emergency or contingency for a long period of time? What happens to the excessive funds in savings? Great question. When savings exceed your three to six months of income goal, take a lump sum out of savings and put it into your investment accounts. However, never ever disrupt the dollars going to savings each pay period to ensure you are well prepared to handle your unforeseen need for cash. Be aware that too many dollars in savings can slow your financial asset growth over time. Interest rates on savings are less than 1%, while inflation may be 3% or higher. This means the effects of inflation are causing you to lose purchasing power. Losing purchasing power means a dollar cannot purchase the same amount of goods and services as in the past. An example would be if your monthly grocery bill is $200 and inflation is 3%. The following year you would need $206 to purchase the same items. Your $200 in hand would come up a little short. This scenario amplifies over a longer period of time. Remember the mission for the funds in your savings account(s). Adequate funds in savings are one of the keys to a successful financial plan and are not designed to grow your assets. That's the mission of the third pillar: investments.

WEALTH ACCUMULATION MADE SIMPLE AND EASY

Teach Children to Save

You owe it to your children to teach them the value of a dollar and how to begin saving early in life. Open a savings account for children and let them help fund it with their own money. Children can begin by saving a portion of their allowances, birthday and Christmas gifts, and later on money earned during their teenage years. Children will enjoy watching the money in their accounts grow while at the same time develop a savings habit that will provide them lifelong benefits. I can recall participating in Christmas clubs at the local savings and loan bank when growing up. We could join the Christmas club and had to save at least 10¢ per week. Having an additional $5 in December to buy Christmas gifts was a big, big help. More importantly, it helped shape my lifelong savings and investment habits, which have remained with me throughout my working years.

FDIC Insurance

Your checking and savings dollars are insured against loss when deposited into federally insured banks and credit unions. The Federal Deposit Insurance Corporation (FDIC), an independent agency of the federal government, insures deposits at its member banks. Your money deposited into qualified accounts as listed below at each member bank is insured for up to $250,000 per person.

- Savings accounts
- Checking accounts
- Money market accounts
- Certificates of deposit (CDs)
- Individual retirement accounts (IRAs) and other retirement accounts

Individuals are insured for amounts above $250,000 based on registration and ownership of different types of accounts. Check with your local bank or the FDIC website (www.fdic.gov), for additional information about FDIC deposit insurance and consumer educational programs.

The National Credit Union Administration Share Insurance

The National Credit Union Administration (NCUA) is an independent agency of the federal government and insures share deposits at federally insured credit unions. You must become a member of a credit union to take advantage of the many services credit unions offer. Once a member, your deposits are made in member share accounts. The NCUA provides federal share deposit insurance through its National Credit Union Share Insurance Fund (NCUSIF). The insurance and coverage amounts are identical to the coverage provided by the FDIC as listed above. Check with your local credit union or the NCUA consumer website (www.mycreditunion.gov) for additional information about NCUA deposit insurance and consumer educational programs.

Suggested Action Now: Set up automatic transfers to your savings account(s) and start or increase savings to an appropriate percentage of your income over time.

Chapter 6

Wealth Management Part 1: Investment Goals and Vehicles

Investment is the exciting pillar of a financial plan and is essential to accumulating wealth. Investments just don't grow; investments grow exponentially over time, which makes it simple and easy to accumulate wealth. This is the area where most people fail to put adequate attention early in their working careers to have a reasonable opportunity to accumulate sufficient funds to address all financial issues as needed and accumulate a substantial nest egg by retirement. As you will see in chapter 7, the longer the period of time you have to achieve your goals, the easier it is to achieve them. Establishing goals and time horizons to achieve your goals, wants, and desires should be a part of your financial plan. This will make your financial journey much more exciting.

Investment Goals

An important step when investing your hard-earned money is to establish investment goals. It's okay to set aside dollars for investments and watch them grow. However, it is much more effective to establish midterm and long-term goals and earmark investments to achieve these goals. Your time horizon as to when you want to achieve your goals sets the stage as to how much you should invest to achieve these goals by your desired timeline. In chapter 7, we will take an in-depth look at how to calculate the required investment amounts to achieve your goals in the timeframe desired.

What are some goals most individuals invest to achieve?

Retirement income is one goal that everyone is concerned about. Sufficient retirement income is a concern for most Americans, and you want to get started on this investment goal as soon as practical. You want your investments to work as hard as you do and grow, grow, and grow while you are in the workforce. Once you retire you want to have sufficient investment funds to supplement your fixed retirement income. Some investment goals you may consider are listed below:

- Retirement income
- Mortgage-free home
- Second home
- Children's college education
- Weddings
- Expensive items, such as a grand piano, boat, etc.
- Dream vacations and travel expenses

This list is by no means complete but should get you thinking about future events that require large sums of money. Investing to reach specific goals requires commitment and encourages you to stick with a long-term financial plan and avoid dipping into your nest egg for short-term gratification. After you establish goals, you should give your full attention to implementing a financial planning strategy to accomplish them in the timeframe desired.

Retirement Nest Egg

Your investments will play a major role in your retirement income; the system is designed this way. The change in how retirement pensions are provided today vs. in the past, defined benefit plans (DBPs) vs. defined contribution plans (DCPs), requires workers to contribute toward our retirement. This change in how retirement pensions are provided was a game changer and puts employees in the driver's seat to accumulate retirement assets to supplement fixed pensions. Let's take a closer look at the differences between these two retirement systems.

Defined Benefit Plans and Defined Contribution Plans

Under DBPs, employers provide employees with a pension in retirement for life. Employers provide employees a certain percentage of their incomes in retirement based on a minimum attained age, number of years worked for the company, and other factors. For example, your firm's defined benefit plan may kick in when you turn the age of fifty-five and worked for the company for at least twenty years. The company may promise to pay you a pension equal to 50% of your income for the rest of your life. At thirty or forty years of service, you may qualify for a pension of as much as 70–75% of your salary while in the workforce. DBPs proved to be very costly, and therefore the majority of companies switched from DBPs to DCPs. Fewer companies offer DBPs today, and most offer DCPs.

Under DCPs, employers do not provide retirees with a pension in retirement. Employees are now required to take charge of their retirement nest egg. The goal is to accumulate a large lump sum and use it in retirement to provide a monthly income to supplement fixed pensions, such as social security. DCPs call for both employers and employees to contribute to employees' retirement accounts. Employee contributions play a major role in the value of their accounts at retirement. Employer contributions are not guaranteed even though most employers contribute to employees' retirement accounts on a regular and consistent basis. Companies set up tax-qualified retirement plans (TQRPs) and match a percentage of workers' contributions to their retirement accounts. The key here is employers "match a percentage of workers' contributions." When workers choose not to set aside a part of their income and contribute to their 401(k) or other TQRP retirement plan, the employer may or may not make any employer contributions. This means these employees may end up with very little or nothing in retirement to supplement social security or other retirement benefits.

Tax-Qualified and Nontax-Qualified Accounts

There are two types of accounts you can invest in to meet your intermediate and long-term goals, nontax-qualified accounts and tax-qualified accounts also known as tax-qualified retirement plans (TQRPs). Your investments in nontax-qualified accounts are after-tax investments, and withdrawals above your cost basis are taxable. There are no government-imposed restrictions on how much you can invest or when you can withdraw funds from nonqualified investments. Restrictions in TQRPs limit how much you can contribute, and there are requirements you must comply with for your withdrawals to be tax and penalty free. Failure to comply with TQRP contribution and withdrawal requirements may result in you having to pay tax on your withdrawals and a 10% additional tax or penalty. TQRPs offer powerful tax incentives to encourage you to accumulate assets to augment your retirement income. TQRPs can be individual- or employer-sponsored plans.

Individual Retirement Accounts

Individuals with earned income can set up individual retirement accounts (IRAs) with financial institutions and fund them throughout their working years. IRAs are classified as traditional IRAs (TIRAs) and Roth IRAs (RIRAs). IRAs offer tax incentives and have limits on how much you can contribute and requirements to withdraw funds tax and penalty free. In addition to these restrictions, individuals have to meet income limits to be able to contribute to RIRAs. In 2022, the maximum contribution limit for both TIRAs and RIRAs is $6,000. If you are age 50 or older by the end of 2022, the maximum contribution is $7,000, which includes an additional $1,000 catchup.

Traditional Individual Retirement Accounts

All individuals can contribute to a TIRA if they or their spouse has earned income. Contributions to a TIRA may be full, partial, or nondeductible depending on your tax filing status and Modified Adjusted Gross Income (MAGI). Earnings in your TIRA grow tax deferred regardless of income and tax filing status. You pay tax when you withdraw funds, and the funds are taxed as ordinary income. You do not have to pay tax again on withdrawals of any after-tax contributions made to your TIRA. After-tax contributions become part of your cost basis and are withdrawn tax free. Earnings on after-tax contributions are taxable because the earnings have grown tax deferred and have never been taxed.

In 2022 you can contribute the maximum to a TIRA.

- If you are single, the head of household, or married filing a separate return and did not live with your spouse during the year and are eligible to participate in an employer-sponsored retirement plan
  o If your MAGI does not exceed $68,000, your contributions are fully deductible.
  o The deductible amount phases out if your MAGI is more than $68,000 but less than $78,000.
  o If your MAGI is $78,000 or more, you can contribute the maximum amount to your TIRA, but your contributions are nondeductible.
- If you are married filing a joint return or a qualifying widow(er) and you or your spouse is eligible to participate in an employer-sponsored retirement plan
  o If your MAGI does not exceed $109,000, your contributions are fully deductible.
  o The deductible amount phases out if your MAGI is more than $109,000 but less than $129,000.
  o If your MAGI is $129,000 or more, you can contribute the maximum amount to your TIRA, but your contributions are nondeductible.

- If you are married filing a separate return and lived with your spouse for a portion of the year
  o If your MAGI is less than $10,000, you can deduct a reduced amount of your TIRA contributions.
  o If your MAGI is $10,000 or more, your TIRA contributions are nondeductible.
- If you and your spouse, if filing a joint return, are not covered by an employer-sponsored retirement plan, your contributions are fully tax deductible regardless of income level.

Roth Individual Retirement Accounts

Individuals can contribute to a RIRA if they or their spouse has earned income and meets income requirements. RIRA contributions are after-tax dollars just like your nontax-qualified investments and are nondeductible. RIRA contributions and earnings grow tax free. There are income limits that determine whether you can contribute to a RIRA and the amount you can contribute if eligible. In 2022 you can contribute the maximum to your RIRA.

- If you are single, the head of household, or married filing separately and did not live with your spouse during the year
  o Your MAGI is less than $129,000.
  o The deduction phases out between $129,000 and $144,000.
  o If your MAGI is $144,000 or more, you cannot contribute to a RIRA.
- If you are married filing a joint return or a qualifying widow(er)
  o Your MAGI is less than $204,000.
  o The deduction phases out between $204,000 and $214,000.
  o If your MAGI is $214,000 or more, you cannot contribute to a RIRA.

- If you are married filing separately and you lived with your spouse for a portion of the year
  o If your MAGI is less than $10,000, you can contribute a reduced amount to your RIRA.
  o If your MAGI is $10,000 or more, you cannot contribute to a RIRA.

Your RIRA contributions are not deductible from your taxes, but keep in mind that withdrawals are tax and penalty free as long as you meet established guidelines.

Check with your certified public accountant (CPA) or the Internal Revenue Service website (www.irs.gov) to determine the amount you can contribute to a RIRA and whether your TIRA contributions are deductible from your taxes. If you have taxable income, you can contribute to a TIRA regardless of income level. The deductibility of your contributions depends on whether you are eligible to participate in an employer-sponsored retirement plan and your MAGI. There are income limitations to meet to contribute to a RIRA as outlined above.

Note: see IRS's "Publication 590-A, Contributions to Individual Retirement Arrangements (IRAs)" on the IRS website (www.irs.gov) to review IRA contribution rules and calculate the amount of your reduced contributions if applicable.

Withdrawals from Individual Retirement Accounts and Your Cost Basis

Withdrawals from your TIRAs may consist of both taxable and nontaxable funds. You are not able to pick and choose the type of funds being withdrawn. IRS uses your cost basis and the pro rata rules to calculate the percentage of your TIRA withdrawals that are tax free. Your cost basis is the amount of your lifetime nondeductible contributions you have made to all your IRAs as of December 31st of each year, excluding RIRAs. To calculate your tax-free withdrawal percentage, divide your cost basis by the total value of all your IRAs, excluding RIRAs but including rollovers from pre-tax TQRPs as of December 31st of each year. For example, if your cost basis is

$10,000 and the value of your IRA accounts is $100,000, your pro rata percentage is 10%. This means 10% of all your IRA withdrawals that occurred in the current year are tax free and 90% of the withdrawals will be subject to tax.

Note: You must keep track of your lifetime cumulative nondeductible IRA contributions using IRS Form 8606 each year. Failure to keep the IRS Form 8606 up to date may result in you having to pay tax a second time on nondeductible contributions you made to your TIRA.

Withdrawals from both TIRAs and RIRAs may be subject to tax and penalty if you fail to meet federal withdrawal requirements. For example, withdrawals from a TIRA are taxed but are penalty free if you are at least age 59 ½ when you withdraw funds. Withdrawals from RIRAs are tax and penalty free if you withdraw funds after the age of 59 ½ and you have owned a RIRA for at least five years.

Note: It is important to note that you must own a RIRA for at least five years before making withdrawals to avoid paying a 10% additional tax, also referred to as a 10% penalty. An additional tax is similar to a 10% penalty but is not tax deductible.

Check IRS Publication 590-B, Distributions from Individual Retirement Arrangements (IRAs), on the IRS website (www.irs.gov) to review IRA withdrawal rules before making withdrawals prior to the age of 59 ½.

Employer-Sponsored Tax-Qualified Retirement Plans

As discussed earlier, defined contribution plans have replaced defined benefit plans for the most part. Many employers sponsor TQRPs such as 401(k), 403(b), and other retirement plans designed to assist employees to set aside a part of their earnings and save for retirement income. Defined contribution plans allow for both employee and employer contributions. Employer-sponsored retirement plans allow all employees elective salary deferrals, and employees can defer significantly more funds in employer-sponsored retirement plans than they can contribute to IRAs. Employees can choose to invest in the traditional pre-tax or the after-tax Roth option regardless of income, marital, or tax filing status.

In 2022, the maximum employee salary deferral amount is $20,500. Employees that are age 50 or older by the end of 2022 can defer an additional $6,500 catchup for a total of $27,000. Every employee can choose to defer the maximum to TQRPs. There are many types of employer-sponsored retirement plans, and the contributions and catchup limits differ among the plans. Check with your human resources department or employee handbook to make sure you are familiar with your employer's plan and contribution limits.

Employer Contributions to TQRPs

Employers can contribute to TQRPs and match a percentage of employees' salary deferral contributions. The combined employer and employee contribution limits are noteworthy. For example, in 2022, the

- Maximum combined employee salary deferrals and employer contributions cannot exceed $61,000. Employees who are age 50 or older by the end of 2022 can defer an additional $6,500 catchup for a total of $67,500.

A huge advantage of participating in employer-sponsored retirement plans is most employers match a percentage of employees' contributions generally either 50% or 100% up to a stated percentage of employees' income. Check with your human resources department or the employee handbook to determine if your employer provides matching funds. If so, make sure you are familiar with and understand the rules to receive the maximum amount of employer matching funds. You need to know how much your employer will match. For example, your employer may

- Match up to 6% of your income dollar for dollar. Therefore, you must contribute a minimum of 6% of your income to your 401(k) or other retirement plan account to receive the 6% employer matching funds. A total of 12% of your income would be going into your account.

- Match 50% of your contributions up to 6% of your income. If you contribute 6% of your income, your employer will contribute 3% to your employer-sponsored retirement account. A total of 9% of your income would be going into your account. However, if you contribute only 3%, for example, to your employer-sponsored plan, your employer would only contribute 1.5%. A total of only 4.5% of your income would be going into your account. That's only half the amount available to you, which will significantly reduce the value of your retirement account now and for years to come. Also, by not taking full advantage of the employer matching funds, you are leaving your money on the table in your employer's coffers. Don't leave money on the table. Contribute to your retirement account and take full advantage of employer matching funds.

Employees can choose whether to contribute and the amount to contribute to employer-sponsored tax-qualified plans. However, employees plan participation and minimum contributions to take full advantage of employer matching funds should not be an option; it should be mandatory, but that would be unlawful and unenforceable. Employer matching contributions are very valuable, and you must contribute so you can take full advantage of the matching funds. Employer matching funds are contributed to your account and start growing on day 1, while other investments may take years to reach a 50% or 100% return. Employer contributions are invaluable and stand alone in providing employees with future income security. This is what we call a "no-brainer." Just do it without hesitation. At this point, hopefully you understand the value of taking full advantage of employer matching funds, so let's review the requirements to keep the employer contributions. It's called vesting.

Vesting

Become familiar with your employer's vesting schedule. *Vesting* means when you the employee own employer matching contributions. Check your employer vesting schedule to determine when you will be 100% vested. Once you are 100% vested, you will own the entire amount of employer contributions in your employer-sponsored retirement account and immediately own all future employer matching contributions. Depending on your employer's vesting schedule, you can be 100% vested in as few as three years of employment and must be 100% vested after the completion of six years of service. If you terminate employment, for example, before you are 100% vested, you will forfeit or give back employer contributions, which exceed your vested percentage. Employees always own 100% of their employee contributions.

Employers will generally use one of two types of vesting schedules, cliff vesting or graded vesting, with many different variations as to how they count employee service. For example, a year of service may be counted as twelve consecutive months in which the employee worked at least one thousand hours or some other requirement. Employer vesting schedules can range from employees being fully vested immediately, after three years of service, or up to a maximum of six years of service.

- *Cliff vesting* means employees will be fully vested no later than at the end of the third year of service. This may mean employees are not vested at all for the first two years and 100% vested at the end of three years or some other variation. Employers' vesting schedules may allow employees to be fully vested sooner than three years of service.
- *Graded vesting* means employees will be fully vested no later than at the end of the sixth year of service. This may mean employees are 0% vested in year 1 and are 20% vested in years 2–6 or some other combination or variation. The key is employees must be fully vested by the end of year 6.

Employers' vesting schedules may allow employees to be fully vested sooner than six years of service.
- All employees must be fully vested by the time they reach full retirement age.

Withdrawals from Employer-Sponsored TQRPs

To comply with federal statutes, employer-sponsored retirement plans have rules established that outline when withdrawals or distributions are allowed. Most plans allow withdrawals or distributions for retirement, death, disability, financial hardship after you reach the age of 59 ½, and many other qualified reasons. Qualified distributions can be lump-sum or periodic payments as authorized in the employer plan.

Early distributions prior to the age of 59 ½ may result in withdrawals being taxed as ordinary income and a 10% additional tax or penalty. If you need to make a withdrawal from your employer-sponsored plan, check with your human resources department or employer-appointed plan administrator to get the facts before submitting a request for early withdrawal. Try not to withdraw funds from your retirement account prematurely and let the funds grow for use in retirement. Follow the financial plan guidelines outlined in this book and put yourself in a good financial position and avoid the emergency need to use retirement funds for other than intended purposes.

Amount You Should Invest

A question at this point may be, How much should I invest? The short answer is to invest as much as you can afford to invest without putting undue stress on your budget and monthly cash flow. Consider investing at least twice as much as you are saving as a minimum. If you are saving 5% of your income, strive to get to 10% or more going to investments. The amount going to investment is a goal, and you may not be able to invest this amount at first. Continue to increase your investments as you pay off debt and dedicate a portion of each pay raise to your financial plan.

Investment Vehicles

Another question may be this: Where do I start investing first? Do I start investing in nonqualified or tax-qualified investments? The general and broad answer is it depends on many factors, such as your family situation, needs and tax status, etc. However, let's just keep it simple; you should start funding your employer-sponsored retirement plan account first, if available, to take full advantage of employer matching funds before starting other investments. Once you are taking full advantage of employer matching funds, start a nonqualified investment in a mutual fund. This way you can allow your retirement funds to grow uninterrupted and at the same time have funds available for midterm goals, such as children's education, weddings, etc.

Professionally managed investments provide significant benefits and are the place to start your investment journey. You should consider investing in stock mutual funds and employer-sponsored retirement plans (401(k)s, 403(b)s, etc.), which are professionally managed. Professional managers and their teams make investment decisions based on sound investment principles.

Mutual funds are the ideal investment vehicles for beginner and midterm investors. Mutual funds provide asset allocation and diversification, which are excellent strategies to use when investing. *Diversification* can be defined as "not putting all your eggs in one basket." *Asset allocation* is applying the right mix of different investment vehicles, such as stocks, bonds, and cash. Mutual funds invest your dollars in many different industries and quality companies within those industries to take advantage of diversification. Mutual funds invest in many industries so that if one industry is down, another industry may be up to provide balance to the portfolio of investments.

Select a mutual fund family and stick with the mutual fund family for the long term. Picking a quality mutual fund family is paramount to a good investment experience. Today is your lucky day because there are numerous quality mutual fund families in the United States. Also, according to Statista,[1] in 2020 there were 7,636 mutual funds in the United States to choose from. So there's a fund or two for everyone. You can find comprehensive information on mutual funds and mutual fund families' ratings and rankings in many national magazines and periodicals. Morningstar (www.morningstar.com) is an industry leader and provides some of the most comprehensive performance data on mutual funds. However, let's keep your mutual fund family selection simple and easy. Look at the fund families your employer has selected for your 401(k) or other employer-sponsored TQRP. Your employer has dedicated significant resources to finding the right fund families for you to choose from to invest your hard-earned money in the employer-sponsored TQRP. Take advantage of your company's hard work and save yourself the frustration of going through a similar process. Consider investing your nonretirement funds in the same fund families until you are confident to select a fund family on your own or engage a financial advisor who will make a fund family recommendation to you.

Investing all your family investments in the same mutual fund family will benefit you and your family. Your family investments including spouse and dependent children in the same fund family may qualify for breakpoints and rights of accumulation, which means you pay discounted fees if applicable and offered by the mutual fund for all qualified family investments.

Investment Objective

Once you've selected a mutual fund family to start your investments, you need to determine your investment objective and select the right mutual fund for you. Mutual fund investment objectives can be categorized with many different names, but there are basically three different strategies: growth of your investments or capital appreciation, current income today, or some variation or combination of the two.

---

[1] Statista, "Number of mutual funds in the U.S. 1997–2020," Published by F. Norrestad, January 11, 2022.

There are many variations of the three investment objectives. A few examples are listed below:

- Growth—concentrates on investing in stocks that have the potential for significant long-term price increase and capital appreciation. Generally suited for investors with a long-term investment horizon.
- Income—concentrates on investments that provide current income today, such as bonds and stocks with a history of paying dividends consistently. Generally, income-producing investment vehicles are well suited for investors who are retired or near retirement and desire additional income.
- Growth and income—concentrates on moderate growth and will invest in both stocks and bonds, including stocks that pay dividends on a consistent and regular basis. Income-producing vehicles are included to reduce volatility.
- Value—concentrates on investing in stocks the fund manager believes are underpriced or undervalued.
- Aggressive growth—concentrates on maximum growth and capital appreciation. These types of mutual funds are designed for long-term investors and may invest in higher-risk investments.

There are many different variations for you to choose from based on your investment objective. I recommend long-term investors consider investing in growth mutual funds on your own and in employer-sponsored retirement plans.

Risk Tolerance

It is important to assess your risk tolerance, which will assist you to select the appropriate mutual fund. The higher the probability of greater returns also means the higher the probability of greater losses due to the increased risk accepted. You should select an investment vehicle that meets your criteria. Again, let's keep it simple and easy. Do not make or stay in investments if you are stressed about your decision or you can't sleep at night because your investment is bothering you. Investing is a long haul, and you want to be in your comfort zone. Therefore, always consider your risk tolerance before investing. You can access free risk questionnaires online on many investment websites. Also, when you engage a financial advisor, he/she will give you a risk questionnaire to complete to assist in determining your risk tolerance.

Each mutual fund has a prospectus that provides the investment objective, risk, past performance, and expenses associated with investing in the mutual fund. Review the mutual fund objective prior to investing to ensure it meets your requirements. You can access and download mutual fund prospectuses on the fund's website and the Securities and Exchange Commission's website (www.sec.gov) EDGAR database.

Contributing to your employer-sponsored tax-qualified retirement plan and investing on your own are not and should not be gambling. You should use proven investment principles, techniques, and strategies when investing your hard-earned money. There are many tools and time-proven investment strategies to assist you on your financial journey, which we will discuss in the next chapter.

Suggested Action Now: Establish investment goals and select a mutual fund.

Chapter 7

Wealth Management Part 2: Investment Tools and Strategies

Okay, it's time to take flight as we prepare to watch our investments soar. We are at a point where we need to address some of the basic investment tools and strategies you should use to start or enhance your investment journey. While there are numerous investment strategies to use, we will discuss two in great detail. Dollar cost averaging (DCA) and compound interest are very valuable, and you must understand both to take advantage of the opportunities that await you. Dollar cost averaging can assist you to accumulate assets and thus put you in a better financial position. Compound interest enables your investments to grow at a rate that may be unbelievable to many. Let's examine both strategies very closely.

Dollar Cost Averaging Investment Strategy

Dollar cost averaging (DCA) is one of the most profound investment strategies for beginner and midlevel investors. DCA means you invest the same amount of money on a regular interval over a long period of time regardless of what the market does. The goal is to invest your hard-earned dollars using time-proven concepts and strategies and not try to time the market or employ strategies such as day trading, which could be akin to gambling. Your long-term investment strategy should not be a gamble. The DCA strategy is to take advantage of the market's ups and downs. By investing the same amount of money each month, you will buy more low-cost shares as stock prices decline. Your investment strategy is to accumulate as many shares as you can of a quality mutual fund, and dollar cost averaging will assist you to reduce the average cost you pay for the shares. Let's examine the DCA strategy in great detail.

Let's invest a hypothetical $100 per month for ten months where the share price starts at $8 per share, increases to $12 per share, and then drops all the way to $4 per share. We will review our account value at month 11 when the market begins an upward trend and recoups some of its losses and gets back to $8 per share where we got started. The status of our investment account will allow us to determine if we have made a return on our investment. See the DCA chart on page 40.

- The first month we invest $100, and the price of each share is $8. How many shares do we get? Let's see. $100 divided by $8 per share equals 12.5 shares.
- Month 2, the market is going up. When we invest $100, each share costs $10; how many shares do we get? $100 divided by $10 per share equals 10 shares purchased. Now we own 22.5 shares.
- Month 3, the market continues to go up. When we invest $100, the cost of each share is $12. $100 divided by $12 per share equals 8.33 shares purchased. Now we own 30.83 shares.
- Month 4, the market is holding steady, and the cost of shares remains at $12 per share. So when we invest $100, we purchase 8.33 shares again. Now we own 39.16 shares.
- Month 5, the market is going down a little. And when we invest $100, the cost per share is back to $10, so we purchase 10 shares again. Now we own 49.16 shares.
- Month 6, the market continues to drop and is back down to $8 per share where we started, so we purchase 12.5 shares again. Now we own 61.66 shares.
- Month 7, the market continues to decline. When we invest $100, the shares cost $6 per share. $100 divided by $6 per share equals 16.66 shares purchased. Now we own 78.32 shares.

- Month 8, the market continues to decline. When we invest $100, the share price is $4 per share, so we purchase 25 shares. Now we own 103.32 shares.
- Month 9, the market remains stable. When we invest $100, the share price remains at $4 per share, so we purchase 25 shares again. Now we own 128.32 shares.
- Month 10, the market begins to increase. When we make our tenth and last investment, the cost of shares is $6 per share again, so we purchase 16.66 shares. Now we own 144.98 shares.
- Month 11, we don't invest, and the market continues its upward trend and is now back to $8 per share where we started. Let's review the status of our account.

We invested $100 ten times, so we invested a total of $1,000. When we add up the number of shares we own, we own a total of 144.98 shares of a quality mutual fund. See the DCA chart on page 40. Each share is worth $8. The value of our account is 144.98 shares times $8 per share equals $1,159.84. When we subtract our initial $1,000 investment, we have a profit of $159.84, a 15.9% return on our investment. How is this possible? We bought many more low-cost shares when the market was down, which reduced our average cost per share. Let's take a closer look at how we made a profit in this market that appears that we should have broken even.

We invested $1,000 and own 144.98 shares. Therefore, our average cost per share is $1,000/144.98 = $6.90 per share. The current value of each of our shares is $8, but we paid an average cost of $6.90, $1.10 less per share. Multiply $1.10 by 144.98 shares. It equals our profit of $159. Please note amounts are not exact due to rounding. At the peak of the market when we invested $100, each share cost $12, so we purchased 8.33 shares. At the market low point when we invested $100, each share cost $4, so we purchased 25 shares or three times as many as we did at the peak of the market. We purchased a lot of shares when share prices were lower. DCA does not guarantee a profit, but it is an invaluable investment strategy to use to accumulate wealth.

The key to DCA is to select a quality mutual fund that provides professional management and invest consistent amounts over a long period of time regardless of what the market does. DCA assists you to take advantage of market fluctuations. You will purchase many more shares when share prices are lower. Once purchased all the shares have the same value in your account regardless of what you paid for them. The lesson learned here is to continue to invest when the market declines because you will purchase more shares when prices are low. Yes, your account value is worth less in down markets, but don't panic; you benefit significantly in down markets by continuing to purchase more low-cost shares of quality mutual funds. Remember it is more difficult to generate a profit when you buy high and sell low. The strategy is to buy low and sell high or at least purchase as many low-cost shares as you can in down markets to offset the high-cost shares in your investment portfolio. Therefore, don't try to time the market; stick to dollar cost averaging.

This short-term extreme market volatility is used for demonstration purposes only, and actual market fluctuations may differ. One takeaway is the market fluctuates but continues an upward trend over the long term. The DCA investment strategy can assist you to benefit from these market fluctuations.

Dollar Cost Averaging Chart

Month	Invested	Share Price	Shares purchased	Total shares	Account Value
1	$100	$8	12.5	12.5	
2	$100	$10	10	22.5	
3	$100	$12	8.33	30.83	
4	$100	$12	8.33	39.16	
5	$100	$10	10	49.16	
6	$100	$8	12.5	61.66	
7	$100	$6	16.66	78.32	
8	$100	$4	25	103.32	
9	$100	$4	25	128.32	
10	$100	$6	16.66	144.98	
11	0	$8		144.98	$1,159.84

One key to wealth accumulation is to acquire quality shares at an average cost less than the market price as we just discovered. Dollar cost averaging does not guarantee you will make a profit. It is, however, a valuable tool to use to accumulate quality shares and take advantage of the ups and downs of the market. To fully understand the value of dollar cost averaging, we must address the value of compound interest.

Compound Interest

Compound interest is another tool you need to be aware of and is vital in accumulating wealth. You receive "interest" in savings accounts in banks and credit unions. You will receive "dividends and capital gains" in your investment accounts. The term *compound interest* applies to both. With simple interest, you receive interest on your original investment. With compound interest, you receive interest (dividends/capital gains) on your original investment and interest received and accumulated. For example, you invest $1,000 at 8% simple interest. You will receive $80 at the end of each year. With compound interest, you will receive $80 at the end of year 1. Year 2, you will receive 8% of $1,080, $1,000 original investment plus $80 interest accumulated, $86.40. Now your account value is $1,080 plus $86.40 in interest received in year 2, which equals $1,166.40. Year 3, you will receive 8% interest on $1,166.40 or $93.31, and so forth. Compound interest will enable your investments to grow exponentially over time.

Dividends and Capital Gains

Your investments will grow from three sources: share price increase, dividends, and capital gains. The manager of the mutual fund you choose to invest in will buy and sell shares of stock of many companies, which make up the mutual fund's portfolio of investments. When these companies make a profit, they distribute part of their profit to their shareholders in dividends. When the mutual fund buys and sells shares of companies' stock and makes a profit, they generate a capital gain. The mutual fund will distribute a pro rata share of the dividends and capital gains to your account. When you fill out an application to invest, always select "reinvest dividends and capital gains" to take advantage of the compounding effect. This way, when your mutual fund distributes dividends and capital gains, the funds will automatically be reinvested and used to purchase additional shares of the mutual fund. Therefore, your mutual fund and employer-sponsored retirement plan investments will receive compound interest.

Compound Interest Example

Many people either don't understand or underestimate the value of compound interest and therefore don't necessarily see how a reasonable monthly investment over a long period of time can grow into a substantial estate. Let's take a look at how compound interest can assist you to accumulate wealth. The compound interest charts on pages 43 and 44 provide the compound interest factors for compound interest at a given rate of return over a number of years for both monthly and lump-sum investments. To see how it works, let's invest a hypothetical $100 per month for 30 years at 8%. The monthly compound interest factor for 30 years at 8% is 1,418. This means if you invest $1 per month for 30 years and average 8% compound interest, you will have $1,418 ($1 times the factor 1,418). We invested $100 each month; therefore, we need to multiply $100 by the factor of 1,418 to determine the value of your account. Your account would be worth a whopping $141,800. Now, that's simple and easy.

Let's imagine when we started investing 30 years ago, you invested a hypothetical $1,000 lump sum and let it grow during the 30-year period. We need to look at the lump-sum investment compound interest chart for 30 years at 8% to find the factor. The factor is 10.06. This means each dollar grew to $10.06. We invested $1,000 and therefore must multiply $1,000 by 10.06 to determine the value of this investment, $10,060. Now we must add the $10,060 lump sum to our monthly account value, $141,800, for a total value of $151,860. That's right. Your investments would be worth over $150,000.

Yes, it's just that simple and easy, and anyone can do it. Just imagine for a moment that your average investment over 30 years was $300 per month instead of $100 in the example above. What would be the value of your account? Your account would be worth over $425,000. Are you beginning to realize how you can accumulate a substantial estate by investing over a long period of time? No gimmicks. It's just that simple and easy.

So, if it's that simple and easy, why isn't everyone doing it? First of all, the objective of this book is to demonstrate to everyone how simple and easy it is to reach a much better financial position. Most people just don't know how simple and easy it is to accumulate wealth. Once you realize how simple and easy it is to get to a better financial position, it requires a mindset change. You must learn to live on less than what you earn so you can set aside dollars for your future, period.

Check out the compound interest calculator on the Securities and Exchange Commission consumer website (www.investor.gov).

Compound Interest Chart
Monthly Investments

Year	1%	2%	3%	5%	7%	8%	10%
1	12	12	12	12	12	13	13
2	24	25	25	25	26	26	27
3	37	37	38	39	40	41	42
4	49	50	51	53	55	56	59
5	62	63	65	68	72	73	77
10	126	133	140	155	172	181	201
15	194	210	227	266	313	340	402
20	266	295	328	407	510	573	724
25	341	389	445	588	787	915	1243
30	420	492	580	819	1176	1418	2079

Compound Interest Chart
Lump-Sum Investments

Year	1%	2%	3%	5%	7%	8%	10%
1	1.01	1.02	1.03	1.05	1.07	1.08	1.1
2	1.02	1.04	1.06	1.1	1.14	1.17	1.21
3	1.03	1.06	1.09	1.16	1.23	1.26	1.33
4	1.04	1.08	1.13	1.22	1.31	1.36	1.46
5	1.05	1.1	1.16	1.28	1.4	1.47	1.61
10	1.1	1.22	1.34	1.63	1.97	2.16	2.59
15	1.16	1.35	1.56	2.08	2.76	3.17	4.18
20	1.22	1.49	1.81	2.65	3.87	4.66	6.73
25	1.28	1.64	2.09	3.39	5.43	6.85	10.83
30	1.35	1.81	2.43	4.32	7.61	10.06	17.45

Investing Your Hard-Earned Dollars

Are you excited yet about the wealth accumulation opportunities that are available to you? Okay, your confidence is growing, and now you have a positive mindset and are confident you can accumulate a substantial estate over time. Another question may be, Should you invest in a TIRA or RIRA, traditional or Roth option in employer-sponsored plans? Let's take a brief detour from the general data I can provide you and keep your decisions simple and easy. Consider whether you prefer to pay taxes on your monthly contributions or the end value of your account. For example, earlier we invested a hypothetical $100 per month for 30 years. We invested $100 per month times 12 (12 months in a year) times 30 (number of investment years), which equals $36,000 in total investment. The account was worth $141,800. In a TIRA or traditional employer-sponsored plan option, you could have deferred the taxes on the $36,000 contributions, but now you have to pay tax on the total $141,800 account value as funds are withdrawn from the account. In a RIRA or Roth employer-sponsored plan option, you couldn't defer the taxes on the $36,000 because you contributed after-tax dollars. However, the total account value of $141,800 is tax free when withdrawn from the account. This simple example would clearly favor investing in RIRAs and Roth options in employer-sponsored plans. Please note this simple example is not a complete comparison because we need to account for the additional dollars that are available by contributing to pre-tax accounts, which reduces your taxable income.

- To continue with the $100 per month investment example, let's assume you're in the 15% tax bracket. $15 (15% of $100 per month) is now freed up each month in the TIRA and traditional 401(k) option, which you can now invest also.
- $15 × 1418 (30-year 8% monthly investment factor) = $21,270.
- Your pre-tax accounts would be worth $141,800 + $21,270 = $163,070 vs. $141,800 in the after-tax RIRA and Roth retirement plan options. You would have to pay taxes on the $163,070 as funds are withdrawn from the pre-tax account. Funds in the Roth accounts will be withdrawn tax free.
- To compare the net values of your accounts, let's take a full withdrawal from both the pre-tax and after-tax accounts without increasing your tax bracket for simplicity purposes.
o Your pre-tax account value is $163,070 × 15% tax bracket = $24,460.50 tax due. $163,070 − $24,460.50 = $138,609.50 net value.
o Your Roth accounts are tax free; therefore, the net value is $141,800.

Please note the net values are similar. Okay, we didn't increase the tax bracket for the pre-tax account even though your tax bracket would have increased had we made a full withdrawal. However, by withdrawing smaller amounts over many years to supplement your retirement income, your tax bracket may or may not increase.

Another factor to consider is the impact of additional taxable income in retirement that may cause you to have to pay taxes on part of or all your social security benefits, increased Medicare Part B premiums, and other taxable factors. So, even with the additional dollars freed up by investing in pre-tax accounts, I recommend you seriously consider investing your IRAs and employer-sponsored plan contributions in Roth accounts.

Backdoor Roth IRAs

Some individuals may not be able to contribute to a RIRA due to their tax filing status and income level. If you are unable to contribute to a RIRA, consider making nondeductible TIRA contributions and then convert the funds in your TIRA account to a RIRA account. Also, many employer-sponsored retirement plans allow employees to convert their traditional pre-tax accounts to Roth accounts. You pay income taxes as you convert the funds from the pre-tax to the Roth account. Once the funds are converted to a Roth account, all the funds in the account grow tax free. Remember all employees are eligible to contribute to the Roth option in employer-sponsored retirement plans without restrictions. And, yes, this process is legal.

Calculating Potential Future Investment Values

Here are a few additional investment tools you can use to assist you to forecast your financial needs and future financial position:

- Use the compound interest tables to assist you to determine how much you need to invest to achieve your established goals at some future point. For example, you want to have $100,000 in 20 years, and you project an 8% return on your investments. Look at the monthly compound interest chart and find the factor for 20 years at 8%, which is 573. Divide $100,000 by the factor of 573 to determine the monthly investment amount required, which is $174.52.

Investing $174.52 per month for 20 years at 8% equals $100,000. That's simple and easy.

- Let's assume you want to accumulate $100,000 in 20 years and you have a lump sum you plan to invest now. Look at the lump-sum compound interest table and find the factor for 20 years at 8%. The factor is 4.66. Divide $100,000 by 4.66 to determine the lump sum investment required today, which is $21,459. Investing a $21,459 lump sum today and letting it grow for 20 years at 8% equals $100,000. That's simple and easy.
- Let's assume you have a lump sum to invest today, but it may not be enough to reach your stated goal. Therefore, you must use a combination of lump sum and monthly investments to reach your goal. For example, your goal is to have $250,000 in 25 years, and you have a lump sum of $10,000 you will invest today. You project your investments will earn 8% based on your mutual fund's actual long-term performance of 10%.
  - First, let's check the lump-sum compound interest chart and find the factor for 25 years at 8%. The factor is 6.85. $10,000 times 6.85 equals $68,500.
  - Next, we subtract: $250,000 − $68,500 = $181,500, to be made up with monthly investments.
  - The monthly compound interest factor for 25 years at 8% is 915.
  - $181,500 divided by 915 equals $198.36 monthly investment required to reach your goal.
  - So investing a $10,000 lump sum today and $198.36 monthly for 25 years at 8% equals $250,000.

This is further evidence of wealth accumulation and goal achievement made simple and easy.

Rule of 72: Describes How Often Your Investments Should Double in Value

The Rule of 72 will give you a ballpark projection of how often you should expect your investments to double in value. The Rule of 72 is widely used among financial services personnel as an indicator or ballpark figure and not a precise projection due to many factors. To calculate, 72 divided by your average rate of return will indicate how long it takes to double your account value. For example, if your investments are averaging 8%, 72 divided by 8 equals 9 years to double your account value without additional investments. For example, today, you have $50,000 in your investments. Nine years later your investments are worth $100,000, nine years (18 years in total) later you have $200,000, and so forth.

I hope you are beginning to see how modest investment amounts over a long period of time can clearly put you in a much better financial position. Put time on your side and get started now.

Important Factors Affecting Your Financial Plan

There are three things you should be aware of to enhance your opportunity to achieve your objectives—time value of money, funding, and rate of return—which are discussed below:

- Time value of money. Don't underestimate the time value of money. The more time you have to achieve your established objectives, the easier it will be to achieve them. People oftentimes find reasons to delay getting started investing. This can be a very costly mistake. Consider this example. When we invested $100 per month for 30 years at 8%, your account value was $141,800. Let's assume you delayed investing for 5 years and only invested $100 per month for 25 years. Let's find the monthly compound interest factor for 25 years at 8% and determine the value of your investment. The factor is 915. $100 times 915 means the value of your account is $91,500. This is $50,300 ($141,800 –

$91,500) less than your account value would have been had you invested for 30 years. You didn't invest $100 per month for 5 additional years, which is $6,000, but your account is worth over a third less. That's the power of the time value of money. You can't make up for not investing in the past, so the best time to get started is *now*. Don't delay getting started. Start investing as soon as practical.

o Let's consider another example to really drive home the superpower of the time value of money. Family A and family B are neighbors and work together. Family A and family B incomes are identical. Family A starts investing $200 per month today and does so for 10 years and stops investing. Family B delays investing for 10 years and then starts investing $200 per month for 20 years. Both families average 8% compound interest on their investments. We will use the monthly and lump-sum compound interest charts to determine the values of their accounts at the end of 30 years.

- Family A invested $200 per month for 10 years at 8% (181 factor), which equals $36,200. Then, the $36,200 lump sum remained invested and averaged 8% for 20 years (4.66 factor), which equals $168,692 total account value at the end of 30 years. Family A invested $200 per month for 10 years, which equals $24,000 in total investment.

- Family B delayed investing for 10 years and then started investing $200 per month for 20 years at 8% (573 factor), which equals $114,600 account value. Family B invested $200 per month for 20 years, which equals $48,000 in total investment.

- *Wow, wow, wow* is the word to be used here. Family A's account value is greater than family B's account value even though family B invested twice as long and twice as much money. In fact, family A's account value is a third more than family B's account even though family A invested half as much as family B: $168,692 – $114,600 = $54,092 difference in account values.

This is a very powerful example of real-life investing; time matters. Hopefully, these examples further clarify the power of time value of money. You must put time on your side and start investing as soon as you can.

- Rate of return. You can't control the rate of return. However, you can select an investment vehicle, such as a quality mutual fund that meets your objective. Many investment firms quote the long-term market return at approximately 10%. Mutual funds are a powerful investment vehicle because mutual funds have professionals managing the funds. The professionals make the buy and sell decisions based on investment principles and strategies. Review the mutual fund prospectus, which includes the mutual fund performance and other pertinent information before investing.
- Funding your investment accounts. You are in complete control as to how much, how often, and how long you invest. The more you invest and the longer period of time your investments have to grow, the more your accounts will be worth. Consider increasing your investment funding as often as you can afford to do so.

Future Funding Increases to Your Investment Accounts

Consider increasing funding to your investments at every opportunity to do so regardless of the amount you allocate to your financial plan initially. So where do you find the dollars to increase your investment funding? Here are a few suggestions:

- Use some of the dollars freed up after paying off loans to increase savings and investment funding.
- Consider using half of each pay raise to increase your standard of living and use the other half to increase funding to your financial plan.
- Consider using a portion of your income tax returns to initiate or increase your savings and investments.

Increase your financial plan funding periodically. You will be glad you did when the immediate need for large sums of cash happens and in retirement.

Investing and Family Priorities and Timelines

After establishing your financial goals and time horizons, prioritize your goals in order of importance. This way you can keep your financial focus on the important goals that matter most to you.

Consider making your retirement income your top priority. When you retire, you can use your investments and savings to supplement your retirement income. While in the workforce, you can recover from cash shortfalls by making more money, working two jobs, etc. In retirement, you will have much less flexibility when living on a fixed income even though you may decide to work at least part-time. Pay raises in retirement, such as your social security benefits and state employee and other pensions, are controlled by and are at the mercy of the federal and state governments or other former employers. Pension increases are usually tied to some index, such as the consumer price index (CPI), and often lag behind inflation over time. Keep in mind you have much less flexibility in retirement unless you have savings and investments owned and controlled by you.

Consider making college funding for children a priority. Start college accounts for children when they are born and fund them at a comfortable rate. For example, $50 per month for 20 years (generally the midpoint of college education) at 8% shows a monthly compound interest factor of 573; $50 × 573 = $28,650. This is an excellent amount of money to assist with college expenses. All your midterm and long-term goals can be funded this way. Remember it is easier to invest $50 or $100 per month over a long period of time than it is to come up with large sums of money when the need for cash is immediate.

Entry-Level Workers

Children need to be prepared to handle their finances when entering the workforce after high school or college graduation. They should enter this phase of their lives with the mindset to live on less than what they make and save and invest money to start their financial journey. The first big step is to participate in their employer's sponsored retirement plan and take full advantage of employer matching funds. Taking full advantage of employer matching funds should not be an option; it's the smart thing to do.

Middle-Aged Adults (Mid-thirties to Mid-fifties)

Middle-aged adults should be settled into their employment and savings and investment habits. Hopefully, you have started amassing a sufficient amount of wealth, retirement, and nonretirement assets. If not, get started now. Let your retirement dollars grow uninterrupted. Nonretirement funds can be used for midterm goals, such as children's education, weddings, etc. Middle-aged adults should save and invest very aggressively in preparation for their retirement years.

Preretirement

Adults in the preretirement stage, ten to fifteen years before retirement, should continue saving and investing very aggressively for retirement. At this stage of life, individuals should begin getting prepared for what's coming next: retirement. Do an analysis of what those retirement years will look like and determine if you will have sufficient income in retirement. Put a plan in place to have a mortgage-free home and be debt free by retirement. A mortgage-free home in retirement is vitally important. If the home is not mortgage free, you will have to make the mortgage payment from your fixed income in retirement, which can have a detrimental impact on your retirement income cash flow and retirement standard of living. Also, take a look at the various company benefits you will lose in retirement and begin replacing the required benefits at the appropriate time to ensure a smooth transition into retirement. For example, do you need to replace employer-provided life and medical insurance? If you retire before the age of 65 before you are eligible for Medicare, you need to purchase health insurance, which may be an unforeseen significant expense. A thorough analysis will help prevent any major surprises as you transition out of the workforce into retirement.

Retirement

Retirement has finally arrived. Hooray! Hooray! It's time to celebrate especially when you have sufficient accumulated assets, a mortgage-free home, and required risk management products in place. You are now free to live an abundant lifestyle. Make sure you are keenly aware of your financial situation, including both lump-sum assets available and monthly cash flow. The question at this point is how to turn a lump-sum investment into a monthly income. That's a great question, one that we will address next.

Retirement Withdrawal Strategy

Well, how do you turn a lump-sum investment into a monthly cash flow to last twenty, thirty years, or even longer? No matter how simple and easy I try to answer this question, this is a complex computation. Turning a lump-sum investment into a monthly income for decades is probably the most disagreeable topic among financial professionals. Many studies have been run to determine how long lump-sum assets will last in retirement. Even though you may receive many different responses to this question, one thing is clear: a long-term sustainable withdrawal rate is 4% or less. Many financial models show success when withdrawing assets at this rate. There is a high probability that lump-sum assets will last at least thirty years in retirement. However, be aware that the appropriate asset allocation is very important at this point, and you should seek the advice of a qualified professional financial planner.

Earlier we demonstrated the value of dollar cost averaging and why it is important to continue to invest consistently regardless of market fluctuations. In fact, we purchased more shares when share prices were lower in down markets. The shares purchased in down markets at lower prices are identical to the shares purchased at much higher prices at the peak of the market; there's no difference. Just imagine if we were liquidating rather than purchasing shares in this scenario. We would have had to liquidate too many quality shares in down markets. While dollar cost averaging works in your favor while investing, dollar cost averaging may not be your friend when you need to make retirement income withdrawals from your investments. Consider this example:

- At the peak of the market when we invested, the share price was $12. At the market's low point, the share price was $4 per share. You are heroes when purchasing quality shares at $4 vs. $12 per share. Now, let's turn our attention to withdrawals.
- Let's invest a hypothetical $10,000 at the peak of the market when investors are excited about the market and share prices are $12 per share. Now, an unforeseen event occurs, and the market goes down to $8 per share. Wow, it may be a great time to invest, but is it a great time to withdraw funds from your investments? Let's take a closer look.
- When you invested $10,000 and the share price was $12 per share, you purchased $10,000/$12 per share = 833.33 shares. Now, you have an immediate need for cash and must withdraw $5,000 from your investments. The current share price is $8 per share. You have to liquidate ($5,000/$8 = 625 shares) 625 shares to withdraw $5,000. So how many shares do you have left? 833.33 (shares originally owned) − 625 = 208.33 shares remaining in your account. So now you own 208.33 shares after making the $5,000 withdrawal from your account. Let's assume the market goes up and now it's back where we invested at $12 per share. You own 208.33 shares at $12 per share, which equals $2,499.96. Your account is now worth $2,500 at $12 per share. Adding the $5,000 you withdrew from the

account, it equals $7,500, which is 75% of your original investment of $10,000. This is a far cry from where you got started. Hopefully, you can see why buying high and selling low is detrimental to your financial future.

This is a very simplistic example to demonstrate a DCA withdrawal strategy. Dollar cost averaging doesn't guarantee a profit; it's a valid strategy for investing but not necessarily in your best interest to use this strategy when withdrawing funds from your account. There are many withdrawal strategies you can use, but it's beyond the scope of this entry-level financial planning book to address them. Okay, I will offer the pros and cons of one simple withdrawal strategy option:

- Take your dividends and capital gain distributions in cash rather than reinvest them.
  o Pros: You do not have to liquidate shares to get cash.
  o Cons: Some years you will receive significantly more money than needed, and in other years you may receive less than needed. What about the impact of compounding when you stop reinvesting dividends and capital gains?

There are pros and cons to every withdrawal strategy. Everyone should be in a position to engage a financial professional before you retire. Consult a professional financial advisor and get help with your retirement withdrawal strategy.

Check out the following government websites to review the many investor tools, calculators, and educational courses available to assist investors with your financial journey:

- Financial Industry Regulatory Authority (FINRA) (www.finra.org). Also, see choosing an investment professional on this website.
- US Securities and Exchange Commission (SEC) (www.investor.gov).

- North American Securities Administrators Association website (www.nasaa.org).

Suggested Action Now: Schedule automatic transfers and start investing now.

Chapter 8

Important Financial Planning Considerations

There are a few additional items we need to discuss briefly to ensure you consider all or most factors affecting your ability to reach a better financial position.

Protecting an Estate

Once you accumulate assets or have dependent children or both, you want to protect the estate to ensure your property and assets are distributed in accordance with your desires.

Will

Everyone should have a will regardless of the size of their estate. In a will, you outline how you want your property distributed and can name a guardian(s) of your minor children if something happens to you. If you die without a will, the states call this dying intestate. Dying intestate means the state will decide what happens to your minor children, assets, and property. The states, a third party, will make decisions that you could have made with a few simple steps. The state may not get it right and do what you would have done under those circumstances. Hopefully, you see the value in getting a will.

Trust

Some families may need a trust. Some family situations are more complex, and estate owners' wishes may need to be addressed in more detail in a trust. A trust goes much further than a will and allows the deceased to "speak from the grave" according to some estate planning attorneys. A trust is a very comprehensive document and allows you to spell out in great detail what you would like to happen in all facets of your estate when you can and cannot speak for yourself. Trusts can alleviate or significantly reduce the need for your estate to go through the very long and costly probate process and third parties to intervene in settling your estate.

Consult an attorney and decide what's in your family's best interest. If you decide you need a trust, work with an estate planning attorney who specializes in estate planning and trusts.

Bringing It All Together

Start a financial plan and address all three pillars: risk management, savings, and wealth management, which translates into investments for beginner and midlevel investors. When you begin your investment journey, jump in with both feet. Don't be detoured by anything from achieving your goals. To succeed, you may have to find work-arounds to make it happen. That's okay. Do it. Be creative and move forward with the taste of financial success in your thinking. Here's an example:

- If you can afford to invest $25 per month and the initial investment calls for $100 minimum, save $25 for four months and invest the required $100.
- If subsequent investment minimums are $50, save $25 per month and invest every two months.

Don't let anything get in your way of getting to a better financial position. Failure is not an option. You must and will succeed. You and your family are counting on your success. Find a way to get to a better financial position one month at a time. This is the mindset I recommend you adopt, and watch your savings and investments grow.

Once you start investing, stay fully invested. Jumping in and out and trying to time the market can be hazardous to your financial future. Financial firms often point out how just missing the ten best trading days or so over decades can have a significant impact on your investment returns. See Fidelity's article "Stay invested: Don't miss out on the best market days" (https://www.fidelity.ca/fidca/en/stayinvested) showing the value of a $10,000 investment in 1986 as researched by Refinitiv[2] from January 1986 to December 2020. If you stayed fully invested, your account value grew to $150,624; if you missed the best ten trading days, the account grew to $48,818; if you missed the best thirty trading days, the account grew to $15,201; if you missed the best sixty trading days, the account grew to $2,933. Do not try to time the market. The facts paint a very clear picture as to why you should stay fully invested at all times regardless of what the market does.

At this point, you have been introduced to the information you need to start a simple but comprehensive financial plan. Whether you choose to do it on your own or engage a financial advisor, do so promptly. Use this book as a reference guide and follow the steps and put your plan in place. I put together a checklist with a few reminders and steps to take to assist you as you begin and continue your long and successful financial journey.

---

[2] Fidelity.ca, Refinitiv, "S&P/TSX Composite index total returns from January 1, 1986, to December 31, 2020."

Financial Journey Checklist

- Develop and maintain a positive mindset that you can and will succeed financially.
- Get a good handle on your budget.
- Manage debt and avoid excessive debt obligations and overextending credit.
- Develop a strategy to pay off debt.
- Pay bills on time to avoid penalties and additional fees. This results in higher credit scores, which means lower interest rates when making loans.
- Start dollars going to savings immediately using automatic transfer to your savings account.
- Address risk management issues as required.
- Establish midterm and long-term goals.
- Start investing in employer-sponsored retirement plans and take full advantage of employer matching funds.
- Start a nonqualified investment in a mutual fund and take advantage of professional management.
- Don't overinvest. Overinvesting is just as bad as under-investing. Why? You won't stick with or sustain such a plan because of the pressure it puts on your monthly cash flow.
- Start education accounts for children.
- Take advantage of the market ups and downs by using dollar cost averaging.
- Use part of each pay raise to increase funding to your financial plan.
- Use a portion of tax returns to enhance your financial plan.
- As you pay off debt, use a portion of freed-up dollars to enhance your financial plan.
- Review your financial plan at least twice per year and make adjustments as required.
- Engage a financial advisor as desired.
- Review appropriate sections of this book periodically as required.

Time to Take Action Now

This book may differ from other books you have read. This book is not to be read and then put on a shelf to look good and accumulate dust. This book is to serve as a guide and reminder of the things you need to do in starting and continuing your journey to a much better financial position. The best and preferred way for you to demonstrate your positive mindset, commitment, and understanding of the teachings in this book is to take action *now*. It's time to stop thinking about it, wishing for it, and dreaming of a better financial life; just get started now. Getting started doesn't mean you have to start saving and investing large sums of money today. In fact, in some cases, getting started doesn't require you to save or invest a single penny today. Getting started does mean you start now addressing the obstacles that will allow you to start or increase your savings and investments in the near future. Most of you are in a financial position now to take action and start or enhance your financial plan. Just do it.

Congratulations! You have finished reading this book. Therefore, you have the basic education and knowledge you need to start your financial journey.

Good luck in your quest for a better financial position. You can do it.

Required Action Now: Start your financial plan.

About the Author

The author grew up in a loving and caring religious environment and learned the value of family, sharing, and the joy of helping others. He started working and saving money at a very young age and purchased his first car at the age of fifteen. He majored in business at the undergraduate and graduate levels because he always had a keen interest in investing and getting to a better financial position. He made his first investment at the age of eighteen and started a comprehensive financial plan at the age of twenty-eight, which he updated periodically throughout his working years.

He joined the financial services industry after retiring from the Air Force and has helped numerous families get started on their financial journey. He saw lots of evidence while in the Air Force and especially as a financial advisor that people need financial education and assistance. He realized it was impossible to help everyone individually. His passion to help others drove him to write this book to reach all working-class Americans.

The author has the highest credentials in the financial services field. He is a recently retired financial advisory firm senior executive with more than twenty-nine years in financial services. He's a financial advisor, certified financial planner, chartered financial consultant, and member of the Financial Planning Association and has many securities and insurance licenses.

The author's mission is to deliver personalized financial services to everyone regardless of current financial status. The author reveals in this book the simple steps you should take to begin or enhance your financial journey.

Printed in the USA
CPSIA information can be obtained
at www.ICGtesting.com
LVHW041331201223
766878LV00056B/736